PRINCEWILL LAGANG

The Future of Work: Entrepreneurship in a Changing Job Landscape

*First published by PRINCEWILL LAGANG 2023*

*Copyright © 2023 by Princewill Lagang*

*All rights reserved. No part of this publication may be reproduced, stored or transmitted in any form or by any means, electronic, mechanical, photocopying, recording, scanning, or otherwise without written permission from the publisher. It is illegal to copy this book, post it to a website, or distribute it by any other means without permission.*

*Princewill Lagang asserts the moral right to be identified as the author of this work.*

*First edition*

*This book was professionally typeset on Reedsy.
Find out more at reedsy.com*

# Contents

1. The Future of Work: Entrepreneurship in a Changing Job...    1
2. The Entrepreneurial Mindset: Building Blocks for Success    4
3. Navigating the Entrepreneurial Ecosystem    7
4. Ideation and Innovation: From Concept to Creation    10
5. Building Your Entrepreneurial Team and Culture    13
6. Business Strategy and Growth    16
7. Financial Management and Sustainability    19
8. Marketing and Branding for Success    22
9. Sales and Customer Relations: The Art of Building...    25
10. Adapting to Change: Resilience and Innovation in...    28
11. Exit Strategies and the Entrepreneurial Legacy    31
12. The Future of Entrepreneurship    34
13. Summary    37

# 1

# The Future of Work: Entrepreneurship in a Changing Job Landscape

The sun dipped below the horizon, casting a warm, golden glow over the city's skyline. The bustling streets, filled with people hustling to get home after a long day's work, served as a stark reminder of the changing nature of employment. The traditional 9-to-5 job, once considered the bedrock of financial security and career stability, was undergoing a profound transformation. In the first chapter of this book, we will explore the evolving job landscape and the role of entrepreneurship in shaping the future of work.

1.1 The Shifting Paradigm

The concept of work, much like the cityscape before us, is in constant flux. The 20th century saw a rise in the industrial age, where people flocked to factories and offices, working for large corporations. The promise of a stable job, benefits, and a pension after decades of service was the Holy Grail of the workforce. But as we moved into the 21st century, the landscape began to shift.

## 1.2 The Rise of the Gig Economy

With the advent of technology, the gig economy emerged, allowing people to embrace flexible work arrangements. Uber drivers, Airbnb hosts, and freelance writers were at the forefront of this revolution. The gig economy offered autonomy and the potential to earn on one's terms, but it came with its own set of challenges, such as job insecurity and lack of traditional benefits.

## 1.3 The Automation Dilemma

As we gaze at the skyscrapers that light up the night, we can't ignore the looming challenge of automation. Robots and AI-powered systems were replacing human workers in various industries, from manufacturing to customer service. The question that hung in the air was whether there would be a place for human workers in the future job market.

## 1.4 The Need for Entrepreneurship

In this era of uncertainty, entrepreneurship emerged as a beacon of hope. Entrepreneurs, those willing to take calculated risks, harness creativity, and innovate, were at the forefront of shaping their destinies. They created their opportunities and defined their work-life balance.

## 1.5 The Entrepreneurial Mindset

Entrepreneurship is not merely about starting a business; it is a mindset, a way of thinking, and an approach to navigating the ever-changing job landscape. This book delves into the essential qualities and skills that make a successful entrepreneur, such as resilience, adaptability, problem-solving, and creativity.

## 1.6 Navigating the Chapters Ahead

As we embark on this journey to explore the future of work and the role of entrepreneurship, each chapter will provide insights, case studies, and practical advice to help you thrive in the evolving job landscape. Whether you are a seasoned entrepreneur or someone considering taking the leap, this book will equip you with the knowledge and tools to succeed.

With the city lights twinkling below, we stand at the precipice of a new era, one that holds both challenges and opportunities. In the following chapters, we will delve into the intricacies of entrepreneurship and guide you towards a brighter, more prosperous future in the ever-changing world of work.

# 2

# The Entrepreneurial Mindset: Building Blocks for Success

As the sun rises over the horizon, it illuminates a new day of possibilities. In this chapter, we delve deeper into the entrepreneurial mindset and the foundational building blocks that underpin success in the world of entrepreneurship.

2.1 The Growth Mindset

Entrepreneurs are driven by a relentless pursuit of growth and improvement. The growth mindset is about embracing challenges, seeing failures as opportunities to learn, and having an unwavering belief in one's ability to adapt and grow. We explore how to cultivate this mindset and apply it to your entrepreneurial journey.

2.2 Risk-Taking and Resilience

Risk-taking is an integral part of entrepreneurship. It's about stepping out of your comfort zone and venturing into the unknown. But every risk carries the potential for failure. Resilience is the ability to bounce back from setbacks, learn from them, and keep moving forward. We discuss strategies for managing risks and developing resilience as an entrepreneur.

2.3 Creativity and Innovation

In the heart of the city's creative district, we explore the importance of creativity and innovation in entrepreneurship. Entrepreneurs are often tasked with finding unique solutions to complex problems. We delve into techniques for sparking creativity and fostering a culture of innovation within your venture.

2.4 Problem-Solving and Adaptability

Every entrepreneurial journey encounters obstacles. Successful entrepreneurs are adept problem solvers who can pivot and adapt to changing circumstances. We examine strategies for identifying, addressing, and even preventing challenges that may arise in your entrepreneurial endeavors.

2.5 Vision and Goal Setting

The cityscape, bustling with activity, serves as a metaphor for the need to have a clear vision and set strategic goals in entrepreneurship. We explore the importance of defining your purpose, creating a vision for your venture, and setting achievable goals to work towards.

2.6 Building a Support Network

Even the most successful entrepreneurs do not navigate their journey alone. Building a support network, including mentors, advisors, and fellow entrepreneurs, is crucial. We discuss how to identify and connect with individuals who can guide and support you on your path.

## 2.7 Cultivating Persistence

The entrepreneurial journey is often a long and arduous one, filled with ups and downs. Cultivating persistence is vital in maintaining the motivation to push forward, even when faced with adversity. We explore techniques for staying persistent and persevering through the challenges.

## 2.8 Overcoming Fear and Doubt

Fear and self-doubt can be significant barriers to entrepreneurial success. We delve into strategies for overcoming these common obstacles and building the self-confidence needed to take risks and pursue your goals.

As the day unfolds, we'll discover how these foundational elements of the entrepreneurial mindset can serve as the bedrock of your entrepreneurial journey. With the right mindset and a commitment to growth, you'll be better equipped to navigate the ever-changing job landscape and build a thriving venture in the face of uncertainty.

# 3

# Navigating the Entrepreneurial Ecosystem

In the heart of the city, where innovation and ambition converge, the entrepreneurial ecosystem thrives. This chapter takes you on a journey through this vibrant landscape, exploring the key components that shape the environment in which entrepreneurs operate.

3.1 Understanding the Ecosystem

The entrepreneurial ecosystem is a complex web of interconnected elements. We'll start by dissecting this ecosystem, breaking it down into its fundamental components, such as government policies, educational institutions, accelerators, and support networks.

3.2 Government Policies and Regulations

Government policies play a significant role in shaping the conditions for entrepreneurship. We'll examine the impact of policies related to taxation, intellectual property, and small business support, and how they can either promote or hinder entrepreneurial activities.

## 3.3 Educational Institutions and Research

Educational institutions serve as nurseries of innovation and entrepreneurship. We explore the role of universities, research centers, and entrepreneurial education programs in nurturing the next generation of entrepreneurial talent.

## 3.4 Funding and Investment

Access to capital is a critical factor in entrepreneurial success. We dive into various funding options, from bootstrapping and angel investors to venture capital and crowdfunding, offering guidance on how to secure the financial resources needed to fuel your venture.

## 3.5 Entrepreneurial Networks

Entrepreneurial success often hinges on who you know as much as what you know. We'll discuss the importance of building strong networks, attending networking events, and forming connections with other entrepreneurs and potential partners.

## 3.6 Incubators and Accelerators

Incubators and accelerators are vital elements of the entrepreneurial ecosystem. We explore how these organizations can provide invaluable resources, mentorship, and guidance to help your venture take off and grow.

## 3.7 Co-Working Spaces and Innovation Hubs

Co-working spaces and innovation hubs have become hotspots for entrepreneurial activity. We'll explore how these environments can foster collaboration, creativity, and access to essential resources, such as shared office space and equipment.

## 3.8 Global Entrepreneurship

In a world where borders are increasingly blurred, we'll discuss the opportunities and challenges of global entrepreneurship. You'll learn how to expand your venture internationally and leverage the advantages of a global market.

## 3.9 Sustainability and Social Entrepreneurship

Entrepreneurship isn't just about profit; it can also be a force for good. We delve into the rising importance of sustainability and social entrepreneurship, exploring how businesses can make a positive impact on society and the environment.

## 3.10 Navigating Challenges in the Ecosystem

While the entrepreneurial ecosystem offers abundant opportunities, it also presents its share of challenges. We'll discuss strategies for overcoming obstacles and thriving within this dynamic and ever-evolving landscape.

As we traverse the entrepreneurial ecosystem in this chapter, you'll gain a deeper understanding of the multifaceted environment in which entrepreneurs operate. Armed with this knowledge, you'll be better equipped to leverage the resources and support available, ultimately enhancing your chances of entrepreneurial success in a changing job landscape.

# 4

# Ideation and Innovation: From Concept to Creation

In the heart of the city's innovation district, where creativity flows freely, we embark on a journey to explore the process of generating and refining ideas, turning them into viable ventures. This chapter delves into the critical stages of ideation and innovation.

4.1 The Art of Ideation

Ideation is the birthplace of innovation. We'll delve into techniques for generating ideas, finding inspiration in the world around you, and fostering a creative environment that encourages ideation.

4.2 Identifying Opportunities

Not all ideas are created equal. We'll explore strategies for identifying opportunities with the most potential, analyzing market trends, and understanding the needs and desires of your target audience.

## 4.3 Validating Ideas

Before diving headfirst into a new venture, it's crucial to validate your ideas. We'll discuss methods for testing concepts, obtaining feedback, and ensuring that your idea has a market fit.

## 4.4 From Concept to Business Plan

A well-structured business plan is the bridge between your idea and a successful venture. We'll guide you through the process of developing a comprehensive business plan, outlining your goals, strategies, and financial projections.

## 4.5 Building a Prototype or Minimum Viable Product (MVP)

To turn your idea into reality, you may need to create a prototype or MVP. We'll explore the significance of these early-stage products and discuss how to build them effectively.

## 4.6 Intellectual Property and Innovation Protection

Innovation often involves the creation of intellectual property, such as patents, trademarks, and copyrights. We'll delve into the importance of protecting your intellectual assets and navigating the legal landscape.

## 4.7 Market Research and Competitive Analysis

Market research is vital for understanding your target audience and competition. We'll provide insights into conducting thorough market research and competitive analysis to fine-tune your approach.

## 4.8 Funding Your Innovation

Innovation requires resources. We'll explore various funding options, from bootstrapping to seeking investors, and offer guidance on securing the necessary capital to bring your innovative idea to life.

4.9 Collaborative Innovation

Innovation doesn't have to be a solitary pursuit. We'll discuss the benefits of collaborative innovation, forming partnerships, and leveraging the expertise of others to enhance your creative process.

4.10 Overcoming Innovation Challenges

Innovation isn't always smooth sailing. We'll address common challenges, such as managing innovation within an organization, dealing with resistance to change, and staying committed to the long-term vision.

As we journey through the process of ideation and innovation in this chapter, you'll gain the knowledge and skills needed to transform your creative concepts into practical and successful ventures. The city's spirit of innovation and creativity will serve as a backdrop to your own journey of turning ideas into reality.

# 5

# Building Your Entrepreneurial Team and Culture

In the heart of the city, where diversity and collaboration thrive, we turn our attention to the vital task of building a strong entrepreneurial team and fostering a culture that drives success. This chapter explores the people side of entrepreneurship.

5.1 The Team Dynamic

Your team is the backbone of your entrepreneurial journey. We delve into the importance of selecting the right team members and creating a dynamic that promotes creativity, synergy, and collective achievement.

5.2 Recruiting and Hiring

The process of finding and recruiting the right talent is a critical step. We'll discuss strategies for identifying the skills, qualities, and values that align with your venture's mission and goals.

## 5.3 Building a Diverse Team

Diversity is a key driver of innovation and success. We explore the benefits of fostering a diverse team and strategies for attracting individuals from various backgrounds and perspectives.

## 5.4 Leadership and Team Management

As the entrepreneur, you'll play a central leadership role. We'll discuss leadership styles, effective team management techniques, and how to inspire and motivate your team to achieve their best.

## 5.5 Creating a Collaborative Culture

Collaboration is at the heart of innovation. We explore ways to foster a culture of open communication, knowledge sharing, and teamwork within your entrepreneurial venture.

## 5.6 Employee Engagement and Retention

Retaining talented team members is crucial. We discuss strategies for engaging and retaining employees, from offering growth opportunities to maintaining a positive work environment.

## 5.7 Handling Conflict and Challenges

Challenges and conflicts are a natural part of any team's journey. We offer insights into how to address and resolve conflicts constructively, maintaining a harmonious and productive work environment.

## 5.8 Remote and Virtual Teams

In an increasingly digital world, remote and virtual teams are becoming more common. We explore the challenges and advantages of managing teams from a distance and offer strategies for effective remote team leadership.

## 5.9 Scaling Your Team

As your venture grows, you'll need to scale your team accordingly. We discuss the challenges and strategies for expanding your team while maintaining the core values and culture of your venture.

## 5.10 Building an Ethical and Responsible Culture

Ethical behavior and social responsibility are becoming increasingly important for businesses. We'll explore how to build a culture that aligns with ethical principles and social responsibility, benefiting both your business and society.

As you navigate the landscape of building your entrepreneurial team and culture, you'll gain insights into the art of team leadership, talent management, and creating an environment that fosters innovation and success. The rich diversity of the city's population serves as a testament to the power of inclusivity and collaboration in achieving your entrepreneurial goals.

# 6

# Business Strategy and Growth

Amid the city's ever-changing landscape, we now dive into the realm of business strategy and growth, where your entrepreneurial journey reaches a critical juncture. This chapter explores the techniques and principles that will help you scale your venture.

6.1 Crafting Your Business Strategy

A well-defined business strategy is the roadmap for your venture's success. We'll delve into the process of crafting a strategy that aligns with your mission, goals, and the evolving market landscape.

6.2 Market Entry and Expansion

Expanding into new markets or segments is a pivotal phase in your entrepreneurial journey. We'll explore various strategies for market entry, whether through organic growth, partnerships, or acquisitions.

6.3 Marketing and Branding

Effective marketing and branding are essential for building a strong presence in the marketplace. We'll discuss how to develop a marketing strategy that resonates with your target audience and creates brand recognition.

6.4 Sales and Customer Relations

Sales are the lifeblood of any business. We'll examine sales strategies, relationship management, and customer retention techniques to ensure the ongoing success of your venture.

6.5 Financial Management

Financial stability is critical for business growth. We'll discuss budgeting, financial forecasting, and strategies for managing your venture's finances efficiently.

6.6 Scaling and Operations

Scaling a business requires careful planning and execution. We'll explore the challenges and strategies for scaling your operations, including optimizing processes, managing resources, and expanding your team.

6.7 Innovation for Sustainable Growth

Innovation doesn't stop at the idea stage; it's a continuous process. We'll discuss how to foster a culture of ongoing innovation to drive sustainable growth in your venture.

6.8 Risk Management

Every venture faces risks, and managing them is essential for long-term success. We'll examine risk assessment, mitigation, and contingency planning to safeguard your business.

## 6.9 Legal and Regulatory Compliance

Compliance with laws and regulations is crucial for maintaining the integrity of your business. We'll explore how to navigate the legal landscape and maintain a responsible and ethical business.

## 6.10 Measuring Success and Adaptation

Success is not a one-time achievement; it's an ongoing journey. We'll discuss key performance indicators, data analysis, and adaptability as tools for measuring and improving your venture's performance.

As we navigate the intricate world of business strategy and growth in this chapter, you'll gain the knowledge and skills needed to steer your venture toward sustainable success in the dynamic cityscape of entrepreneurship. Your entrepreneurial journey, like the city itself, is ever-evolving, and mastering these strategies will empower you to thrive amidst change and competition.

# 7

# Financial Management and Sustainability

In the heart of the bustling city's financial district, we turn our attention to the crucial aspects of financial management and sustainability. This chapter focuses on the foundation of your venture's long-term success, ensuring that it thrives in both good times and challenging moments.

7.1 Financial Planning and Budgeting

Financial planning is the cornerstone of your venture's financial stability. We'll explore the process of creating a comprehensive financial plan and budget to guide your financial decisions.

7.2 Funding and Capital Allocation

Securing and effectively allocating capital are vital for a thriving venture. We'll discuss various funding sources, from loans and investors to grants and bootstrapping, and how to make informed decisions about capital allocation.

7.3 Cash Flow Management

Cash flow is the lifeblood of your business. We'll examine strategies for maintaining a healthy cash flow, managing accounts receivable and payable, and navigating financial challenges.

7.4 Financial Statements and Analysis

Financial statements provide insights into your venture's financial health. We'll dissect income statements, balance sheets, and cash flow statements, and discuss how to analyze these documents to make informed decisions.

7.5 Tax Planning and Compliance

Understanding taxation is crucial for financial management. We'll delve into tax planning, compliance, and strategies for optimizing your venture's tax structure.

7.6 Risk and Contingency Planning

Risk management is essential for financial sustainability. We'll explore strategies for identifying and mitigating risks, as well as developing contingency plans to handle unexpected financial challenges.

7.7 Sustainability and Responsibility

In the heart of the city, we'll discuss the rising importance of sustainability in business. We'll explore strategies for integrating sustainability and corporate social responsibility into your financial management practices.

7.8 Financial Growth and Expansion

Your venture's financial journey doesn't stop at stability; it also includes growth and expansion. We'll discuss financial strategies for scaling your business while maintaining a strong financial foundation.

## 7.9 Financial Literacy and Education

Financial literacy is essential for informed decision-making. We'll provide resources and insights to enhance your understanding of financial management, ensuring that you can make sound financial choices.

## 7.10 Monitoring and Adaptation

Financial management is an ongoing process. We'll discuss the importance of continuous monitoring, adaptation, and alignment with your venture's goals to ensure long-term financial sustainability.

As you navigate the financial landscape in this chapter, you'll gain a deeper understanding of financial management principles, allowing you to build a sustainable and resilient venture. The city's financial district serves as a reminder that, like the stock market, the entrepreneurial journey has its ups and downs, but with the right financial strategies, you can navigate these challenges and thrive in the long run.

# 8

# Marketing and Branding for Success

In the heart of the city's vibrant commercial district, we explore the dynamic world of marketing and branding, crucial components of any thriving entrepreneurial venture. This chapter focuses on the strategies and techniques that will help your business stand out in a crowded marketplace.

8.1 Crafting Your Marketing Strategy

A well-crafted marketing strategy is the roadmap to effectively reaching your target audience. We'll delve into the process of defining your brand, identifying your target market, and selecting the best marketing channels to reach your customers.

8.2 Content Marketing and Storytelling

Content is king in the modern marketing landscape. We'll explore the power of content marketing, storytelling, and how to create compelling narratives that engage and connect with your audience.

## 8.3 Social Media Marketing

Social media has transformed the way businesses interact with customers. We'll discuss strategies for leveraging the power of social media platforms to increase brand visibility, engage with customers, and drive conversions.

## 8.4 Search Engine Optimization (SEO)

Search engine optimization is essential for online visibility. We'll delve into the fundamentals of SEO, including keyword research, on-page and off-page optimization, and how to improve your website's search engine rankings.

## 8.5 Paid Advertising

Paid advertising, including pay-per-click (PPC) and display ads, can be powerful tools for reaching a broader audience. We'll discuss how to create effective paid advertising campaigns that deliver results.

## 8.6 Email Marketing

Email marketing remains a potent channel for connecting with your audience. We'll explore the strategies for building and nurturing an email list, crafting engaging email content, and driving conversions through email campaigns.

## 8.7 Branding and Identity

Your brand is more than just a logo; it's the essence of your business. We'll discuss the importance of branding and how to develop a strong brand identity that resonates with your audience.

## 8.8 Influencer Marketing

Influencer marketing can be a game-changer in reaching a broader audience.

We'll explore how to identify, collaborate with, and leverage influencers to promote your products or services.

8.9 Analytics and Data-Driven Decision-Making

Data is a valuable asset in the world of marketing. We'll discuss how to use analytics tools to gather insights, measure campaign performance, and make data-driven decisions to improve your marketing efforts.

8.10 Adaptation and Continuous Improvement

Marketing is an ever-evolving field. We'll explore the importance of adapting to changing trends, experimenting with new strategies, and continuously improving your marketing and branding efforts.

As you navigate the dynamic world of marketing and branding in this chapter, you'll gain the knowledge and skills necessary to promote your venture effectively, reach your target audience, and build a strong brand that stands the test of time. Just as the city's commercial district is a hub of activity, your marketing and branding efforts will become the driving force behind your business's visibility and success in a competitive marketplace.

# 9

# Sales and Customer Relations: The Art of Building Relationships

In the heart of the city's bustling marketplace, we delve into the art of sales and customer relations, two pillars of any successful entrepreneurial venture. This chapter focuses on the techniques and strategies that will help you not only attract customers but also build long-lasting, meaningful relationships with them.

9.1 The Sales Process

The sales process is the journey from initial contact to closing a deal. We'll explore the key stages of the sales process, including prospecting, qualifying leads, presenting your product or service, handling objections, and closing the sale.

9.2 Sales Techniques and Strategies

Effective sales techniques are essential for converting leads into customers. We'll discuss various sales strategies, including consultative selling, relationship selling, and solution-based selling, and how to apply them to your specific business.

## 9.3 Customer Relationship Management (CRM)

Building and maintaining strong customer relationships are vital for long-term success. We'll delve into customer relationship management (CRM) tools and practices that help you understand and meet your customers' needs.

## 9.4 Building Trust and Credibility

Trust is the foundation of any successful customer relationship. We'll explore strategies for building trust and credibility, including transparent communication, delivering on promises, and consistently providing value.

## 9.5 Customer Experience and Satisfaction

Creating exceptional customer experiences is a competitive advantage. We'll discuss how to exceed customer expectations, gather feedback, and ensure high levels of satisfaction to drive repeat business and referrals.

## 9.6 Handling Customer Complaints and Resolving Issues

Every business encounters customer complaints and issues. We'll provide strategies for handling these situations with professionalism and efficiency, turning dissatisfied customers into loyal advocates.

## 9.7 Cross-Selling and Upselling

Maximizing revenue from existing customers is a key strategy. We'll explore cross-selling and upselling techniques to increase the value of each customer relationship.

## 9.8 Customer Loyalty Programs

Customer loyalty programs can be powerful tools for retaining customers. We'll discuss the creation of effective loyalty programs that incentivize repeat business and foster customer loyalty.

## 9.9 Online and E-commerce Sales

In the digital age, online sales are a significant channel for many businesses. We'll explore strategies for effective online and e-commerce sales, including website optimization, online marketing, and customer support.

## 9.10 Sales Ethics and Responsible Practices

Ethical sales practices are essential for building a positive reputation. We'll discuss the importance of ethical sales techniques and responsible business conduct to maintain customer trust.

As you explore the world of sales and customer relations in this chapter, you'll gain the knowledge and skills needed to create a customer-centric approach to your business. Just as the city's marketplace is a hub of activity, your focus on building strong relationships with your customers will be the driving force behind your business's growth and long-term success.

# 10

# Adapting to Change: Resilience and Innovation in Entrepreneurship

In the heart of the city, where change is the only constant, we explore the pivotal theme of adaptation, resilience, and innovation in entrepreneurship. This chapter delves into the strategies and mindsets required to navigate the ever-evolving entrepreneurial landscape.

10.1 The Need for Adaptation

The entrepreneurial journey is filled with unexpected twists and turns. We'll discuss the importance of adaptability and the ability to embrace change as an inherent part of entrepreneurship.

10.2 Resilience in the Face of Adversity

Resilience is the capacity to bounce back from setbacks and challenges. We'll explore strategies for developing resilience, managing stress, and maintaining a positive outlook even in the most challenging times.

10.3 Learning from Failure

Failure is not the end; it's a stepping stone to success. We'll discuss how to embrace failure as a learning opportunity, extract valuable lessons from it, and apply those lessons to future endeavors.

## 10.4 The Role of Innovation

Innovation is the lifeblood of entrepreneurship. We'll delve into how innovation drives growth, how to foster an innovative culture within your venture, and ways to consistently generate new ideas.

## 10.5 Embracing Technology and Digital Transformation

The digital age offers numerous opportunities for innovation and growth. We'll discuss how to leverage technology and embrace digital transformation to stay competitive and adapt to changing market dynamics.

## 10.6 Evolving Business Models

Business models are not set in stone. We'll explore the importance of continuously evaluating and adapting your business model to remain relevant in a shifting landscape.

## 10.7 Market Trends and Future Forecasting

Staying ahead of market trends is a strategic advantage. We'll discuss the importance of market research and future forecasting to identify emerging opportunities and threats.

## 10.8 Strategic Pivots

Sometimes, a pivot in your business strategy is necessary. We'll explore the art of strategic pivots, how to identify the right time to pivot, and how to execute a successful transition.

## 10.9 Collaborative Innovation and Partnerships

Collaboration with other entrepreneurs and organizations can drive innovation. We'll discuss how to form strategic partnerships, collaborate on projects, and leverage collective expertise for mutual benefit.

## 10.10 The Entrepreneur's Mindset for the Future

As the cityscape changes with the times, so must the entrepreneurial mindset. We'll conclude this chapter by discussing the enduring qualities and attributes that will continue to serve entrepreneurs well in an ever-evolving world.

In this chapter, you'll gain the knowledge and tools needed to not only survive but thrive in a world that demands adaptability, resilience, and innovation from entrepreneurs. Just as the city's landscape changes with the seasons, your ability to adapt and innovate will determine your long-term success in the entrepreneurial journey.

# 11

# Exit Strategies and the Entrepreneurial Legacy

In the heart of the city, where the legacy of entrepreneurs is etched into the skyline, we explore the essential topic of exit strategies and the enduring impact of entrepreneurship. This chapter focuses on the final stages of your entrepreneurial journey, including the legacy you leave behind.

11.1 The Importance of Exit Strategies

Every entrepreneurial journey has an endpoint. We'll discuss the significance of exit strategies, whether it involves selling the business, passing it on to a successor, or simply moving on to new endeavors.

11.2 Preparing for a Successful Exit

Preparation is key to a successful exit. We'll explore the steps and considerations involved in preparing your business for a transition, including evaluating your financials, legal matters, and operational readiness.

## 11.3 Selling Your Business

Selling your business can be a complex process. We'll discuss strategies for finding the right buyer, negotiating a fair deal, and ensuring a smooth transition to new ownership.

## 11.4 Succession Planning

Passing on your business to a successor is a significant decision. We'll delve into succession planning, including how to identify and groom a suitable successor within your organization or family.

## 11.5 Retiring as an Entrepreneur

Retirement is a new beginning. We'll explore how to transition into retirement gracefully, manage your finances in retirement, and explore new passions and pursuits.

## 11.6 Leaving an Entrepreneurial Legacy

Entrepreneurship is about more than just profits. We'll discuss how to leave a lasting legacy, whether through charitable giving, mentorship, or contributing to causes that matter to you.

## 11.7 Navigating Emotional Challenges

Exiting a business can be emotionally challenging. We'll provide insights into managing the emotions, such as a sense of loss or uncertainty, that can arise during the transition.

## 11.8 Reinventing Yourself

Entrepreneurs are often driven by a desire for continuous growth. We'll explore how to reinvent yourself, embrace new challenges, and find fresh opportunities after your exit.

## 11.9 Contributing to the Entrepreneurial Community

Many successful entrepreneurs find fulfillment in giving back to the entrepreneurial community. We'll discuss ways to contribute your expertise, mentorship, and resources to support aspiring entrepreneurs.

## 11.10 The Enduring Impact of Entrepreneurship

As the city evolves, the impact of entrepreneurship endures. We'll conclude this chapter by discussing the lasting influence and contributions that entrepreneurs make to their communities and the world.

In this chapter, you'll gain insights into the art of planning for your exit from the entrepreneurial world, whether it's through a successful sale, a seamless transition to a successor, or a well-earned retirement. Just as the city's skyline tells the story of generations of entrepreneurs, your exit strategy and entrepreneurial legacy will be a testament to your journey and the impact you've made.

# 12

# The Future of Entrepreneurship

In the heart of the city, where innovation and ambition continue to shape the landscape, we turn our gaze to the future of entrepreneurship. This final chapter explores the evolving trends, opportunities, and challenges that entrepreneurs are likely to encounter in the years to come.

12.1 Shaping the Future

The future is an open canvas for entrepreneurs. We'll discuss how entrepreneurs can actively shape the future through their innovations and visionary leadership.

12.2 Emerging Technologies

Technology is at the forefront of the future. We'll explore the impact of emerging technologies such as artificial intelligence, blockchain, and biotechnology on entrepreneurship and how entrepreneurs can leverage these innovations.

12.3 Sustainability and Social Responsibility

Sustainability and social responsibility are central to the future of entrepreneurship. We'll discuss the increasing importance of environmental and social sustainability and how businesses can be a force for positive change.

## 12.4 Globalization and Market Expansion

The world is becoming increasingly interconnected. We'll delve into the opportunities and challenges presented by globalization and the strategies entrepreneurs can use to expand their ventures globally.

## 12.5 The Gig Economy and Remote Work

The way we work is evolving. We'll explore the gig economy, remote work trends, and how entrepreneurs can adapt to changing work structures and create opportunities in these emerging areas.

## 12.6 Diversity and Inclusion

Diversity and inclusion are driving innovation and growth. We'll discuss the benefits of fostering diverse and inclusive workplaces and how entrepreneurs can lead the way in creating more equitable businesses.

## 12.7 Regulatory and Legal Landscape

As the business world changes, so do regulations. We'll discuss the evolving regulatory and legal landscape and how entrepreneurs can stay compliant and adapt to new requirements.

## 12.8 The Entrepreneur's Role in Society

Entrepreneurs have a significant role to play in shaping society. We'll explore the social and ethical responsibilities of entrepreneurs and how they can contribute to the betterment of their communities.

## 12.9 Lifelong Learning and Adaptation

Continuous learning is a key to staying relevant. We'll discuss the importance of lifelong learning, staying adaptable, and embracing change as an integral part of the entrepreneurial journey.

## 12.10 The Next Generation of Entrepreneurs

The future of entrepreneurship lies in the hands of the next generation. We'll conclude this chapter by discussing how experienced entrepreneurs can mentor, guide, and inspire the emerging generation of business leaders.

As you navigate the uncharted territory of the future of entrepreneurship in this chapter, you'll gain valuable insights into the trends, challenges, and opportunities that will shape the entrepreneurial landscape in the years to come. Just as the city continues to evolve and transform, the world of entrepreneurship remains dynamic and full of possibilities for those who embrace change and innovation.

# 13

# Summary

"Entrepreneurship: Navigating the Ever-Changing Landscape" is a comprehensive guide divided into twelve chapters that cover the entire entrepreneurial journey. It delves into essential topics such as the entrepreneurial mindset, ecosystem, ideation, innovation, team building, financial management, marketing, customer relations, adaptation, exit strategies, and the future of entrepreneurship. Each chapter provides valuable insights, strategies, and real-world advice to help aspiring and established entrepreneurs thrive in the ever-evolving world of business.

This guide not only offers practical guidance for building and scaling a successful venture but also emphasizes the importance of ethical practices, social responsibility, and leaving a positive entrepreneurial legacy. It underlines the enduring impact entrepreneurs can have on their communities and society as a whole.

As the city serves as a backdrop, symbolizing constant change and growth, the guide encourages entrepreneurs to adapt, innovate, and shape the future of entrepreneurship. It emphasizes the importance of continuous learning, adaptability, and the mentorship of the next generation, underlining that entrepreneurship is an ever-evolving journey with opportunities, challenges, and transformative potential.

www.ingramcontent.com/pod-product-compliance
Lightning Source LLC
LaVergne TN
LVHW020457080526
838202LV00057B/6000